HOW TO PLAY

ELECTRIC

GUITAR

A Beginner's Guide to Learning the Electric Guitar
Basics, Reading Music, and Playing Songs with Audio
Recordings

any advice or information presented, whether for breach of contract, tort, negligence, personal injury, criminal intent, or under any other cause of action.

You agree to accept all risks of using the information presented in this book.

You agree that by continuing to read this book, where appropriate and/or necessary, you shall consult a professional (including but not limited to your doctor, attorney, or financial advisor or such other advisor as needed) before using any of the suggested remedies, techniques, or information in this book.

Table of Contents

How to Play Electric Guitar

This is a book for anyone who wants to take their first steps into the world of this amazing instrument. In it you will find information about the electric guitar including its parts, functioning, history, and a review of famous players who will give you the confidence to start your journey.

We'll discuss the basic aspects of understanding and playing this instrument, such as correct posture, tuning, tablature reading, chords, and exercises for both hands.

Finally, I invite the student to enjoy this process, have patience, and practice. The electric guitar is a wonderful instrument and your work will be rewarded if you have discipline. Let's move on.

Every time you see this symbol next to an exercise it means we have recorded it for you and you can listen to it when you practice.

Please follow along with the recordings at the Sound Cloud link below or search on Sound Cloud for "How to Play the Electric Guitar".

https://soundcloud.com/jason_randall/sets/how-to-play-the-electric-guitar

An Introduction to Electric Guitar

In this section you'll learn about the electric guitar and its parts, functioning, history, and evolution. The first step to becoming a great guitar player is learning the basics. So, let's begin!

The Electric Guitar

Do you know what an electric guitar is? Yes, it's a guitar that you plug in and play Rock and Roll with, but how would you define it?

An electric guitar is a musical instrument made of metal strings (usually 6, but there can be up to 12). It is a versatile instrument that can generate a multitude of sounds and styles thanks to the possibility of distortion and alteration offered by its configuration and the pedals that typically accompany it. These characteristics allowed for the evolution of Jazz, Blues, Rock, and all their subgenres.

The electric guitar functions based on the principle of electromagnetic induction, which converts the vibrations of its metal strings into electrical signals. This process is done through microphones or pickups that receive these vibrations and transform them into electrical signals capable of being amplified and processed.

Electric guitars

Because the generated signal is weak, it is amplified before being sent to a speaker. This output signal can be altered through electronic circuits to modify aspects of its sound. It can also be modified with effects such as reverberation and distortion.

The most important parts of an electric guitar are the pickups, because they are responsible for transforming the vibrations of the strings into electricity, so it can reach the amplifiers and everyone can hear it.

Some guitars don't have a sound box (solid electric guitar) or have a smaller sound box than usual (semi-solid). These may have holes to the outside with "f" shapes similar to those of violins and other acoustic instruments.

Pickups

It's important to note that the sound produced by this instrument is altered depending on the material used in its manufacture (wood, acrylic, etc.), the construction process of the instrument (fretting, tuning and octavación), and the quality of the pickups.

History and Evolution

In the previous segment, we discussed the basic functioning of the electric guitar. Now you'll learn about this instrument's fascinating history and evolution.

In 1920, two situations gave rise to the creation of the electric guitar, sparking a musical revolution. After the end of WWI began a period known as the "Jazz Age" during which Jazz bands gained popularity in the United States. This created a need for a new sound and higher guitar volume, since the guitars of the time could not be heard at concerts. At the same time, the radio industry developed electric amplification.

These two conditions were propitious, for in 1923, Lloyd Loar, engineer of the Gibson Guitar Factory, created the first electric microphones, now known as pickups. He came up with the idea to add them to the acoustic guitars of the time to enhance their sound at Orchestral Jazz concerts.

In 1928, the company Stromberg-Voisinet offered the first electric guitar commercially, with a pickup like the one created by Loar connected to the soundboard. However, they could not create a signal strong enough.

A few more years passed before the electric guitar achieved an adequate volume. In 1931 the "Frying Pan" was commercialized in the United States by George Beauchamp and Adolph Rickenbacker. In addition to looking like a frying pan, this guitar was played on the knees, had no sound box, and had pickups on the body. Today this guitar costs about €2500.

Frying Pan

In 1935, Leo Fender, a radio repairman, took advantage of the appearance of the amplifier to create the first electric guitars. These were solid with removable necks and few pieces, so it was easy for players to change pieces of the instrument.

It wasn't until 1950 that the first electric guitar went on the market. The Fender Broadcaster was a commercial success. So good was its reception that in 1954 the second model came out, the Fender Stratocaster, possibly one of the most famous in history.

Fender Broadcaster 1950

With these inventions began the worldwide commercialization of the electric guitar. Since then, many brands have made a name for themselves: Gibson, Fender, Les Paul, Epiphone, and others.

Earlier History

Historical instruments similar to electric guitar

Before the invention of the electric guitar, the acoustic guitar had been in existence for more than 4,000 years. This historical instrument must be treated with respect.

Archaeologists have discovered the remains of string instruments such as the arpabol and the tambur, as well as a "guitar" used by the Egyptian singer Har-Mose. It is believed that the guitar evolved from the lute or the zither. This was one of the noblest instruments of Ancient Rome. However, this information cannot be verified.

Since then, the guitar has undergone many transformations, finally leading to the appearance of the electric guitar in the twentieth century.

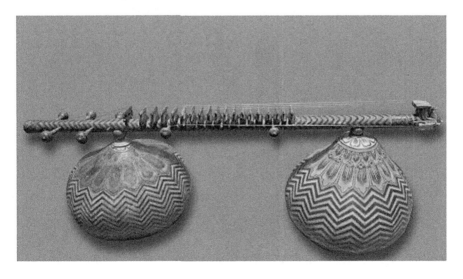

Zither

Guitar Parts and Kinds of Guitars

Parts of the Electric Guitar

Electric guitars are made up of many parts including the head, the neck, the body, the bridge, and the pickups.

Electric Guitar Parts

The Body

One of the essential elements of the guitar is its body. It consists of several parts including the pickups and the bridge. Let's learn about each of these.

Pickups

Without pickups, it would be impossible to detect the vibrations made by the strings of the guitar and transfer them to the amplifier to amplify the sound. An electric guitar can have between one and three pickups, usually separated from each other by a few centimeters.

The pickups are basically six magnets surrounded by a thin copper wire. This wire is thinner than human hair and surrounds the magnets 7200 times.

There are many types of pickups, each with their own peculiarities, but in general, they're classified into two groups: single coil pickups and double coil pickups, or humbuckers. The sounds of these are very different, each with their own characteristics. If there is one thing that defines the sound of your guitar more than anything else, it is the type of pickups.

Bridge

The bridge is a small piece located below the pickups that holds the strings in the correct places. The attachment of the strings can vary according to the guitar model. Currently there are "no vibrato," or fixed bridges and "vibrato" bridges such as floating and semi-floating bridges.

Fixed bridges provide stability for tuning, since the bridges do not incorporate any type of mechanism that could detune the instrument like the tremolo bar. They are limited to holding the strings, modifying their height, and adjusting the calibration.

On the other hand, floating and semi-floating bridges are mobile bridges that allow us to modify the tension of the strings and perform a vibrato effect when the lever is operated. The floating bridge can be operated both forward and backward and is able to loosen or tighten the strings.

Semi-floating bridges are not suspended, but rest on the wood of the guitar's body. They loosen the strings and return them to their original position.

Pickup Selector Switch

The pickup selector switch is in the body of the guitar. It allows you to choose between bass and treble depending on what you want to play and what effects you want. Some guitars allow you to use both at the same time.

Volume and Tone Controls

These buttons are located on the body and are used to determine the sound level and tone of the guitar. You can also adjust the sound with the amplifier.

Input Jack

The input jack is where the plug that connects the guitar to the amplifier goes.

Strap Button

This small hook is used to attach the strap to the instrument.

Tremolo Bar

The tremolo bar is located on one side of the bridge and produces an effect or distortion on the tone signal of the guitar. It can make the sound more severe, more acute, or both, depending on the type of guitar.

The Neck

Now that you know what's in the body, let's look at the elements of the neck, where you press the strings to play chords.

Fretboard

The fretboard is the piece of wood that covers the neck on which the strings of the guitar are pressed. The length of the fretboard may vary depending on the guitar. Classical guitars usually have a shorter fretboard than electric guitars.

Frets

These are the lines that are distributed by the fretboard. The fingers should be placed near the frets to properly press the strings and avoid producing a lot of vibration, unless you like vibrato.

Fret Markers

These are small samples, which are located on the neck in the form of points, squares, or triangles, to help the guitarist locate himself. These are generally located in frets 3, 5, 7, 9, and 12.

Strings

Most guitars have six strings. The upper one is the most severe and the lowest one is the sharpest. The strings exert pressure on the neck to keep it straight.

Head

The head is in the upper part of the guitar; on it you can adjust the strings to adapt your tension level.

Tuners

These tune the strings when turned. The more you tense the guitar, the sharper it will sound.

Nut

This part plays an important role in the vibration of the strings. The nut is located between the head and the neck. Made of hard nylon, it prevents the strings from vibrating beyond the neck. The strings must be placed in their small slots.

Truss Rod

The truss rod is a metal bar that is inserted into the neck and helps adjust its curvature to compensate for the tension exerted by the strings. To regulate this, it can be accessed through a screw located on the head of the guitar. On the neck are two tensions, that of the strings and that of the truss rod, which help to counteract the strength of the strings.

Kinds of Electric Guitars

There are several types of electric guitars that vary in their characteristics, like strings, pickups, body, and bridge. We'll learn a little more about this in this section.

Types of Bodies

As with classical guitars, electric guitars can have different bodies that produce different sounds.

Hollow Body

Hollow body electric guitar: GIBSON ES 150

When talking about the electric guitar, we often imagine a guitar with a compact drawer with no space inside. However, some electric guitars have a hollow body.

Some musicians prefer this kind of box for its heavier sound. In addition, the sound resonates more easily. These guitars are used by Jazz fans. They have two f-shaped holes similar to those of violins. This is the case for the Gibson ES 150.

Solid Body

Solid body electric guitar

These guitars, called solid body guitars, appeared in the 50s. These are mainly appreciated by rockers because they have no retroaction effect on the sound and can control it more easily.

Semi-Hollow Body

Semi-Hollow body electric guitar

As with pickups, some guitars combine the two types of sound boxes. This adds acoustic resonance to the sound without favoring the effect of feedback at high volumes.

Types of Bridges

Bridges play an important role in the accuracy of the instrument. Although we already talked about them in the previous section, we will now delve a little deeper into their typology. There are two types of bridges for the electric guitar.

Fixed Bridge

Fixed bridge

This is the most common type of bridge. As its name indicates, it cannot move because it's fixed in the soundboard. Given its immobility, it's impossible to change the pitch of the notes that are played. The advantage of a fixed bridge is that the strings are better maintained and not as easy to adjust.

Floating Bridge

Unlike a fixed bridge, a floating bridge can be moved with the help of a tremolo bar. Moving the bridge from top to bottom allows the height of the notes to be varied. To get more serious notes, simply move the bridge up, and move it down to get higher notes.

Floating bridge

This system is used mostly by Hard Rock and Heavy Metal groups.

Brands of Electric Guitars

Today, there are many outstanding brands that occupy an important place in the world music market. We'll discuss a few of them in this section.

Fender

In 1940, Leo Fender created his own shop of electronic repairs and manufacturing. Today, this company is one of the most famous in the world of electric guitars and amplifiers.

Gibson

The Gibson Guitar Corporation was founded in 1902 by Orville Gibson, who was a fan of the mandolin. Today it is one of the largest guitar manufacturers in the world. The Gibson is recommended to get the best sounds and effects on the electric guitar.

Epiphone

Epiphone guitars, both electric and acoustic, are generally known for their good prices. These offer good sound quality and are a favorite of beginners.

Ibanez

Many stars have an Ibanez. These guitars are famous for their quality and their exceptional and original design.

Vigier

This is a French company whose guitars are considered high-end.

Effects for Guitars and Pedals

In the previous chapter you learned about the anatomy, typology, and characteristics of the electric guitar. Now we'll discuss the sounds you can make with your guitar and/or the pedals you connect to it. If you're a beginner, you might wonder why your guitar does not sound the same as your favorite Rock icon. Here you will learn how these effects are achieved.

Sound Effects of the Electric Guitar

The effects or "signal manipulations" of the electric guitar are alterations in its tone or sound. Effects can be produced by physical causes, such as natural reverberation, or by processors intended to fulfill a specific function in the signal, such as pedals.

The concept of signal manipulation began in the 1940s, when artists began to experiment with saturation. At the time, the guitar amplifiers were low fidelity and only produced distortion by mistake. It was considered something that should be repaired immediately.

In the 1950s, guitarists from all over the world began to make these "mistakes" voluntarily by altering or "damaging" their amplifiers to sound different. Later, the first pedals were created.

The rest of the effects arose from different forms of recurrent manipulation in sound. In the 60s and 70s, the most recognized companies producing multi-effects and pulsating pedals were born, and several brands brought their innovations to the market.

Effects and Pedals

Your electric guitar can produce more than 20 effects. These effects are grouped into sets according to their characteristics. A few examples are saturation, which affects the level of sound gain, modulation, which alters the sound based on the amplitude, frequency, and phase of a signal, equalization and dynamics, which allow you to control the tone of your guitar in a more detailed way, space or environment, which simulate different room sizes, and tempering, which allows you to change the sound frequency.

You can find a pedal that executes each of these effects or a multi-effect pedal. Next, we will delve into the pedals of saturation, ambience, and modulation effects.

Effects Pedals

Saturation effects

Overdrive: Moderately affects the second harmonic, which generates irregular peaks in the signal. The tones are focused on the low and medium. The sound is considered "dirty," but the fundamental note is distinguishable and the saturation is not very hard, so it still makes a natural guitar sound.

The overdrive pedals give us a saturation boost, coloring the sound strongly in many cases, and giving us the warm sound of the hot valves. Think of the sound of Stevie Ray Vaughan to get an idea. There are several types, the most famous being the Tube Screamer that Ibanez commercialized in the early 80s and that was designed and manufactured by Maxon. These usually have three controls: output level, tone (more acute or severe), and gain level.

Fuzz: Similar to the overdrive, but its effects are more exaggerated. The signal peaks are generated in greater intensity. The sound is very dense, with little sharpness. It seems that a defective mixer was the "culprit" of the birth of the Fuzz.

Its name is onomatopoeic - Fuzz refers to the buzz that surrounds the sound of this saturation.

Famous guitar players who used Fuzz are Jimi Hendrix, Carlos Santana, Keith Richards, Eric Johnson, Robby Krieger, Matthew Bellamy, Josh Homme, George Harrison, Paul McCartney, and John Lennon. Its controls vary a lot depending on the manufacturer, but generally you will find an output level and a fuzz level.

Distortion: The second and third harmonics are enhanced. The signal is saturated, the fundamental note is indistinguishable, and the wave is irregular. High mid tones stand out, although with higher distortion, there is also notable bass. The sound is dirty and pleasant to the ear.

The distortion pedals are much more powerful and usually more acute than the overdrives. With these, high gain sound is sought. These are almost exclusively used by Metal groups.

Environment Effects

Reverberation: Effect based on the repetition of signals with a delay. However, the purpose of reverb is not to produce differentiated repetitions of the original signal to generate an echo effect, but rather it is something subtler that produces the sensation of being in a cave, a tile basin, or a metallic tank.

The more reverb we apply to the signal, the more "big room" sensation we get. In Surf Music the reverb goes to the top, and in Trash Metal it tends to be almost zero.

Delay: The multiplication and delay of a sound signal. Once processed, the signal is mixed with the original. The result is the classic echo effect. In any simple delay pedal you can find buttons to regulate its operation, like the level of delay, feedback, and mixing.

In more advanced models you can find controls such as frequency drop over time, adjust several different echoes, MIDI synchronization, and frequency filtering.

Modulation Effects

Chorus: This effect mixes and superimposes two signals, one of them in constant vibration, and one detuned and delayed in low measure with respect to the first.

The result is the sound of two instruments playing in unison, so one of them tunes slightly. It was exploited in the 80s and has been used by several famous guitarists like Steve Lukather, Zakk Wylde, Kurt Cobain, and Gustavo Cerati.

There are controls for frequency and rate adjustment and the level of mix, tone, and pre-delay.

Flanger: As with the chorus, the signal is doubled, detuned, and delayed, but the delay time of this one is much smaller. It emerged as a flaw in tape recordings on open-coil tape.

It produces a metallic oscillating sound, especially in medium and high frequencies. It was used and popularized by Eddie Van Halen and Andy Summers, who made it part of his label in the legendary band The Police.

Amplifiers

The amplifiers are almost as important as the electric guitar or the pedal because that's where the sound comes from. They're designed to amplify an electrical signal of sound emitted by the guitar so it is produced through a loudspeaker. Most amplifiers can modify the tone of the instrument by emphasizing or attenuating certain frequencies and adding effects such as distortion and reverberation. There are three types of amplifiers.

Valve Amplifier or Tube Amplifier

These are built with vacuum tubes, also called lamps, valves, or bulbs. You must use these at full volume to appreciate their sound quality.

Tube amplifiers are much more sensitive to the musician's touch and to the type of guitar. The sound is considerably varied from one way of playing to another. In addition, they offer a sound that is often described as "vintage," which is characterized by having a unique distortion, greater warmth, and a feeling of being louder. These are heavier, require more maintenance, are more expensive, and require a warm-up.

Transistors Amplifier

These are also called solid state amplifiers and are built by transistors. They're comfortable, light, and do not require a warm-up. They offer a more controlled and flat response. However, it should be noted that in recent years, the technology in this class of amplifiers has developed considerably, and today these are able to emulate the sound of tube amplifiers.

In addition, this type of amplifier sometimes incorporates other effects, so they offer greater versatility at a lower price.

Hybrid Amplifiers

Hybrid amplifiers combine valves and transistors, offering a sound and response halfway between the two, with less cost and maintenance than the tube amplifiers, and with greater dynamic range. What we want to achieve is the natural, warm tone of the valves, while reducing costs and inconveniences.

Tuning and Metronome

Tune Your Guitar

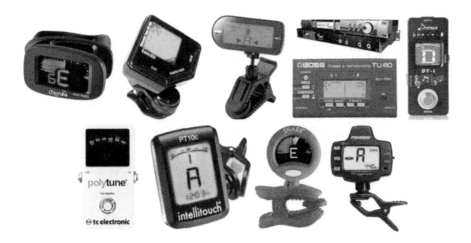

How to Tune the Guitar

Once you know which musical note each string corresponds to, you can tune the guitar. Many beginners do not know how to tune their guitar and should ask for help. Knowing how to tune is a requirement. If the guitar is not tuned, the music you produce will not sound good. There are several ways to tune a guitar. These are the most common:

- Using acoustic and manual tuners as a tuning fork

- With electronic tuners, which measure the sound frequencies of the strings

- With some instrument like a piano or keyboard

- With a smartphone application

- Using a video with reference notes on YouTube

It is advisable to always carry your tuner in your guitar case. It will provide you with at least one reference note that you can use to tune the strings.

For example, striking a tuning fork produces the sound of an A (frequency of 440 Hz), with which the 5th string of the guitar can be tuned.

Relative Tuning Method

Once you have tuned one of the strings with a reference note, you can tune the rest of them. The goal is to compare the sound of the strings and make them sound the same. This is how I tune my guitar:

- The 6th string on the 5th fret should sound the same as the 5th string in the air.

- The 5th string on the 5th fret should sound the same as the 4th string in the air.

- The 4th string on the 5th fret should sound the same as the 3rd string in the air.

- The 3rd string in the 4th fret should sound the same as the 2nd string in the air.

- The 2nd string on the 5th fret should sound the same as the 1st string in the air.

- The 1st string in the air should sound the same as the 6th string in the air.

Almost all comparisons are made by pressing the strings on the 5th fret, but to fine-tune the 2nd string the comparison is with the 3rd string on the 4th fret.

What If I Don't Have a Tuner?

It's common for friends to ask us to play the guitar when we're not ready. If you don't have anything available to tune your guitar with, don't worry. Choose a reference note and follow the previous method. What matters is that the guitar sounds good. If there are two guitars, refine one first and use it as a reference to refine the second one. If you're a beginner, you can use the tension of the string as a reference. Try not to over-tighten the 5th string. Once you decide that the tension is adequate, tune the rest of the strings.

With time and practice you will memorize the sound of some of the strings and tune without the need of a device.

Play Track 1

In case you do not have a tuner, we have included a track with the notes of the guitar, so you can use them as a reference and tune at home.

Metronome

In this section you'll learn how to use a metronome and incorporate it into your daily practice to become a better guitarist.

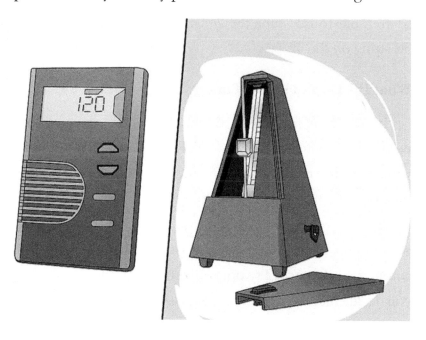

What Is a Metronome?

A metronome is a device used to indicate the tempo. It emits an acoustic or visual signal that allows us to maintain a constant tempo.

The metronome was invented around the year 1800. Until that time, composers didn't have any device with which to measure the speed of their songs. Therefore, they could not tell the performers how fast to play.

It is believed that Beethoven was the first to use a metronome. He wanted people to reproduce his music at the tempo he had imagined.

You can currently find electronic, mechanical gadgets, smartphone applications, and computer software to use as a metronome.

Beats per Minute

The term beats per minute, or BPM, is used to establish the duration and speed of musical figures accurately. The duration of the sound is defined and how many of these figures (quarters) we can find in a minute.

If the metronome is set to 80, it will sound 80 BPM. If you set it to 60, it will sound 60 BPM, or one every second.

All the exercises in this book rely on a metronome, so be sure to get one.

Reading Chords, Diagrams, and Tabs

How to Read the Chord Diagram on the Guitar

The chord diagram is a way to write chords on the guitar. Each vertical line is a guitar string: E in the 1st string, B in the 2nd string, G in the 3rd string, D in the 4th string, A in the 5th string, and E in the 6th string.

We will also have horizontal lines, which are the frets, and the nut of the guitar, which is represented by a "0".

Once you have understood the mechanics you will not mind the position in which the diagram is and if it is more or less aesthetic, since you will understand if perfectly, come as it may.

Example:

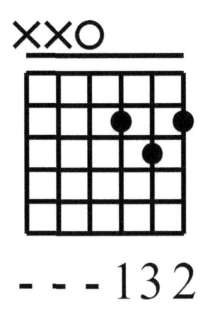

The diagram is another way of teaching the chords; a drawing is more accessible to some people because it doesn't feel as much like having to memorize music.

In this figure, we see the neck in a vertical position. The six vertical lines represent the strings, where the one on the left is the thickest string and the one on the right is the thinnest.

The spaces between the horizontal lines are the frets (in this case the top one is the first). The numbers on the bottom indicate the fingers you have to press on. Each string is numbered like this:

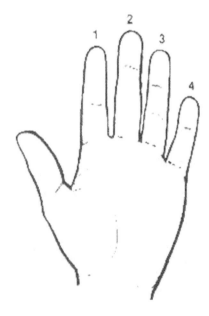

They are numbered the same, whether from the left or right hand. The dashes in the lower part indicate that the strings do not touch any finger (they touch the air or they do not touch at all).

The "X" at the top indicates that strings do not have to be touched. The "O" indicates that the strings of which they are playing open (without pressing any frets). The black dots tell us what string and fret to press. When you get used to the logic of the diagrams, you will begin to understand them perfectly.

How to Read a Tab

Here we'll go through four steps to read guitar tabs. Remember that you can always come back to this chapter to review the components of tablature reading. Let's start!

What Is Tablature?

Tablature is a graphic representation of a guitar. It has six horizontal lines that represent the six strings of the guitar. The first line at the top is the sharpest string and the last line is the lowest string.

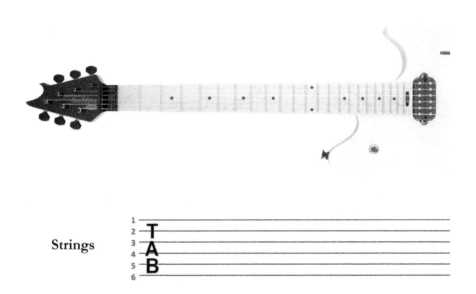

Strings

The Frets Are the Numbers

Just remember that the guitar has frets and these are represented by a number on the line or string that we want. This will indicate the fret that we must tread.

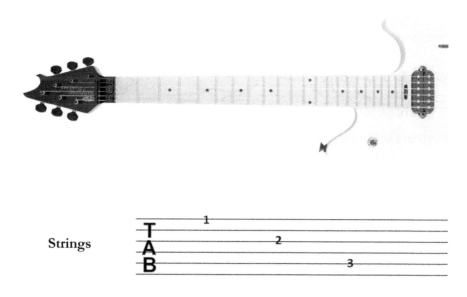

If we have a zero in any line of the tablature, this indicates that we do not have to press any frets, just touch the string in the air.

If the numbers are followed one behind the other, it means that each note is played after the one you have already played.

If you see one note on top of the other, this means that you play them at the same time, like when you play chords. Here is an example of the A minor chord in tablature:

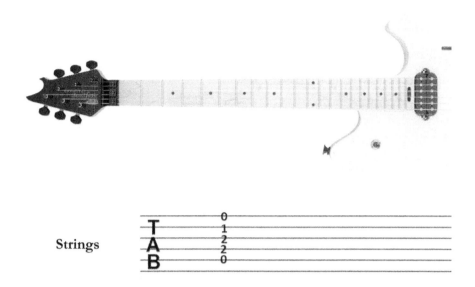

Strings

You will often find a tablature written in another way, but for practical purposes it is the same.

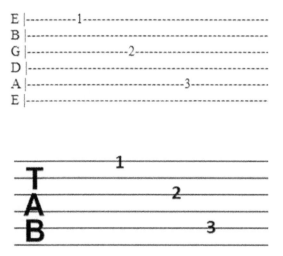

This happens because many people who upload tabs to the internet do so without using sheet music editing software.

The Musical Figures and Their Values

Music is not just sounds, it is also duration. In this lesson you will learn to distinguish the value of musical figures in a 4/4 time signature as well as their silences.

With this explanation, you can draw your own conclusions for the other binary measures such as 2/4 or 6/8.

The Measure Unit

To understand them, let us look at an example of one of the most common measures in music, the 4/4 time signature. In the 4/4 time signature, the denominator, or second number of the fraction, indicates that there are different notes that can fit in it or different musical figures that can complete it.

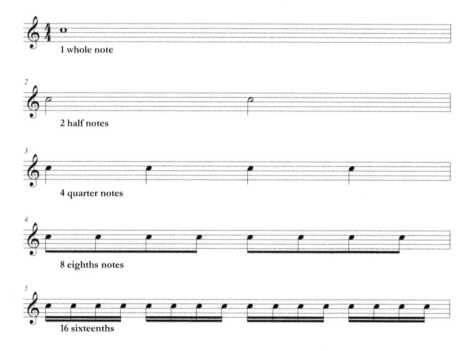

That is, to complete it, the total sum must give 4 Beats, with which, the notes can be mixed. While the numerator is also 4, which represents the unit of measure.

Examples of combinations:

- Half note + 2 quarter notes

- Quarter notes + 4 eighth notes

- 8 sixteenth notes + 4 eighth notes

The Unit of Time

The unit of time is marked by the numerator, or the first number of the fraction. It tells us that the figure that completes a beat is the quarter notes one. Here you must think about the isolated notes, not the measure.

In 4/4, each type of note has its value:

- Whole note = 1 (occupies 4 beats)

- Half note = 2 (occupies 2 beats)

- Quarter note = 4 (occupies 1 beat)

- Eighth = 8 (occupies 1/2 beat)

- Sixteenth = 16 (occupies 1/4 beat)

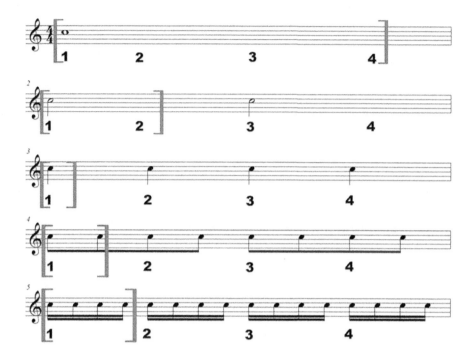

The quarter note tells us that according to the measure (4/4), it indicates what the unit of time is. Therefore, musical figures larger than the quarter note, such as whole note and half note, do not fit within a single beat.

The figures that are shorter, like the eighth notes and sixteenth notes, fit within the line of music, but require more notes to complete the line of music.

The Notes and Their Silences

Let's discuss the values of the musical figures above and their respective silences. Keep in mind that the stem, that is, the note stick, can be placed up or down and does not affect the duration of the musical notes.

Whole Note

This note is represented as a circle on the staff. Its duration is equal to four beats in a measure of 4/4. It would fit only one whole note or a whole note silence. The silence of a whole note obviously has the same value.

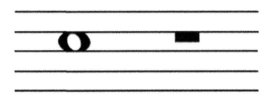

Half Note

This note is represented as a note with a stem on the staff. Its duration is equal to two beats in a measure of 4/4. That means only 2 half note or 2 half note silences would fit.

Quarter Note

The quarter note is represented as a black dot with a stem in the pentagram. Its duration is equal to 1 beat in a measure of 4/4. That means it would only fit 1 quarter note or a quarter note silence on a beat and 4 quarter notes or 4 quarter note silences in a measure.

Eighth Note

This is represented as a quarter note with a stem and a bracket on the staff. Its duration is equal to a half beat in a measure of 4/4, meaning it would only fit 4 quavers or 4 quaver rests in a beat.

Sixteenth Note

This is represented as a quarter note with a stem and 2 brackets. Its duration is equal to a quarter beat in a measure of 4/4. That means it would only fit 4 sixteenths or 4 silences of sixteenths in one beat and 16 sixteenths in one measure.

It's important to know the values of musical figures to understand how music is measured. In the past, there was no way to transmit sound with as much accuracy as we can now with scores, recorders, and computers. It was thanks to the Catholic Church and its liturgies in the Middle Ages that musical notation has evolved into what it is today.

Tablature With and Without Rhythm

There are tabs that set the rhythm below and tabs that do not. The disadvantage of those that do not mark the musical rhythm is that you have to know the song in advance to be able to play it. On the other hand, if you have a tablature with rhythm, you do not need to know the song because you already know the values of the musical notes.

Tablature with rhythm

Tablature without rhythm

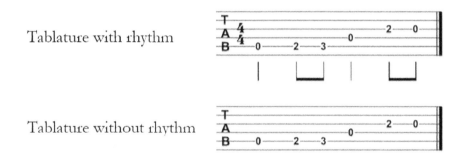

Below the numbers you have the stripes that represent a quarter note followed by two eighth notes joined together. If you know the values of the notes, you will know how to interpret this.

If you're going to play something from a tablature without rhythm, try to make it a song that you already know.

Notation and Nomenclature

The guitar is a versatile instrument with which we can create many effects and techniques and for that reason, we have had to create some symbols to represent them in the tablature. These are the most used techniques and how they are written:

a) Pick Down/Pick Up

They come out above or below the numbers in the tablature.

Pick Down   **Pick Up**

b) String of Chord

It is a vertical wavy line that tells us that we have to strum the chord.

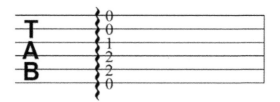

c) Hammer On

It is represented with a ligature or an "h" depending on the tablature.

d) Pull Off

It is also represented with a ligature or a "p."

```
_____          ----------------------
_____          ----------------------
_____          ----------------------
-------11⌒-----9--------          ------11p9-------
_____          ----------------------
_____          ----------------------
```

e) Slide

This is a line between both numbers; it tells us that we move from one note to another by sliding the finger.

```
_____          ----------------------
_____          ----------------------
_____          ----------------------
-------3----5-----------          ------3/5---------
_____          ----------------------
_____          ----------------------
```

f) Bend

The bend is represented by an angled arrow and a symbol above that tells us how much we have to bend. If you see 1/2 it is a semitone. Regarding the other script, the bend appears in it with the fret indicated and the note that is reached with the "bend" in parentheses. It sometimes appears with a number followed by a "b" and then the other number.

g) Vibrato

This is represented by a wavy, horizontal line above the number. It tells us that we have to make the string vibrate.

Many more advanced techniques are represented on the tablature, such as pre-bend, forced harmonics, tapping, dive bomb, gargle, violin effect, and sweep picking. However, we will not discuss those in this lesson because they're not as commonly seen by beginners as the ones mentioned above.

Body Posture and Correct Hand Position

Body Position

The electric guitar is designed to be hung by a strap or belt, partly due to its weight, since it can be made of solid wood, and partly because its shape differs from that of a traditional guitar.

Although the electric guitar is meant to be played standing, I recommend studying while sitting. The weight of the instrument will be felt in the shoulders, neck, and back, creating tension.

The best position to learn to play the guitar is sitting, with the guitar resting on the left leg, which will be somewhat raised (rest it on something that will raise it a few inches), and with the head of the guitar at shoulder height.

I recommend that you use the strap of the guitar when you're sitting, and that you use it in such a way that if you get up, the guitar is in the same position as it was when you were sitting.

It is also common to put the guitar on the left leg, but this makes it more difficult to reach the last frets of the last strings and to position the little finger well.

Try not to vary much from the recommended position, especially when learning, because your technique will suffer.

Pick and Right Hand

Grip the Pick

Have your hands outstretched. Flex your index finger on itself, place the pick pointing with the tip towards the nail, and put your thumb on top.

Draw a kind of circle between the thumb and the index finger. This way, the pick will be well anchored on the surface of the fingers and it will be less likely to fall.

The most common mistake is to hold the pick with the tips of the fingers. By not having enough support, it can fly away at some point.

Your grip must be firm, but not too firm, because with each strike of the pick there is a struggle between the tension of the string and the tension of the pick. If neither of the two yields, the pick will get stuck, because the string is not very flexible and probably will not yield.

There are many types of picks with different calibers and materials. I recommend that you try several, so you can see which one suits you best.

Exercises to Improve Pick Control

Play Track 2

For this series of exercises, we will set the tempo of our metronome to 100 BPM, or *Play track 2*, which is a pre-selected track of a metronome at 100 BPM.

In this chapter you are going to learn an exercise that will make you more comfortable with the pick. These exercises must be done at least three or four times a day. If you practice consistently, you will see results.

First, put the hand that goes on the neck over the strings without pressing them, so they will remain muted. Note the movement of the pick, which is described in the chapter "Notation and Nomenclature," and which is located at the top of the tab.

You can listen to these exercises in tracks 3-7 in the audio tracks included.

Exercise 1

Play Track 3

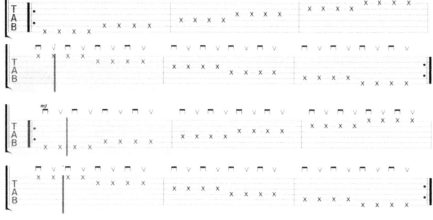

Exercise 2

Play Track 4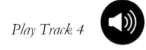

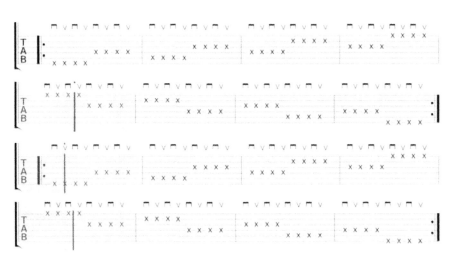

Exercise 3

Play Track 5

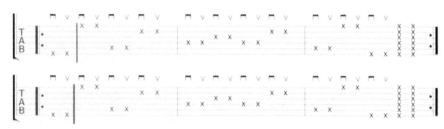

Exercise 4

Play Track 6

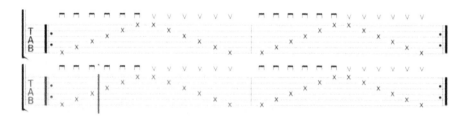

Exercise 5

Play Track 7

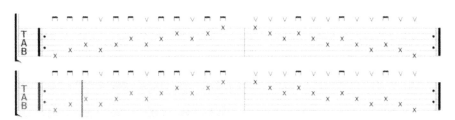

Melodies and Left Hand

We're going to discuss three important concepts: speed, precision, and hand strength.

The first piece of advice I am going to give you is not to compress and decompress your fingers. The idea is that the movement is made through a block and that no irregular movement occurs in the hand. There must be an equal distance between the tips of the fingers - about half a centimeter. Remember to move the whole block of the hand when required.

The second piece of advice is that for no reason should you lift the fingers of the fingerboard excessively. There are people who do this without noticing. To develop speed, you have to economize the movement of your fingers. If your fingers are too far away from the fretboard, they will take more time to return to the strings. Always try to keep a short distance between the fingerboard and your fingers - one centimeter or less.

Playing slowly will help you learn correct finger placement. When you play slowly, you give your brain a chance to recognize the movements so that you can eventually do them quickly. That is why we learn to crawl before we learn to walk. The practice must to be slow to start moving fast.

Make sure you understand the rhythms and accents before executing an exercise. Try to keep time with your shoulders, head, or foot. Always try to maintain a proper tempo and correct symmetry.

Exercises to Improve Fingering

This first exercise is quite simple. It is important to put your finger in the middle, and not on the neck or too low. Your thumb and hand should be arched to prevent any possibility of hurting them.

Exercise 6

Play Track 8

If these exercises tire you, rest your hand, lower it, and shake it a little. When you feel rested, begin the practice again. Pain is never a sign that you are doing it right.

This second exercise is about agility. Fingers three and four are not naturally nimble; they are a bit stupid and clumsy. The point of this exercise is to make these two fingers get along well with each other. Once you get the hang of this exercise, many licks that you have to play with these two fingers will not be as hard.

Exercise 7

Play Track 9

Many fingering exercises for newcomers are based on one string, but unfortunately no one in the guitar world plays one string all the time. It is essential to do exercises to master two strings.

Exercise 8

Play Track 10

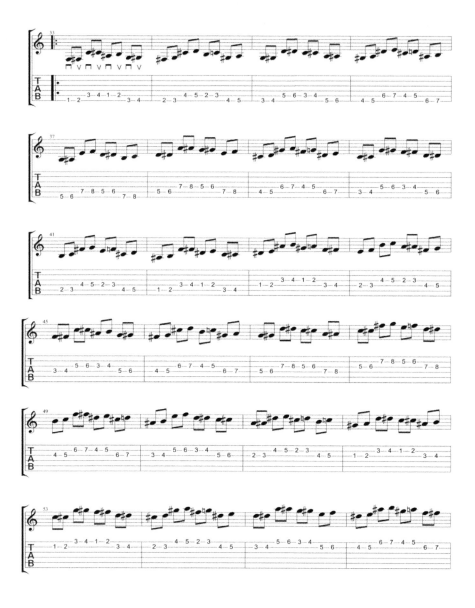

Exercise 9

Play Track 11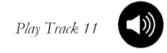

Playing Chords

Major and Minor Chords

To begin with, work with two types of chords - major chords and minor chords. Major chords are represented by a capital letter:

A, B, C, D, E, F, G

Minor chords are represented by a capital letter accompanied by a lowercase "m":

Am, Bm, Cm, Dm, Em, Fm, Gm

The major chords are characterized by an energetic and happy sound, while the minor chords have a sad, closed sound without as much energy. With these basic chords you will be able to play any song you want.

Barre Chords

The barre chords are based on the so-called open chords, because they use the nut of the guitar to make notes, without having to step on any fret (open notes).

When we want to play those same chords in a position closer to the body of the guitar, we will have to use our index finger to sound the notes that the nut was responsible for in an open chord.

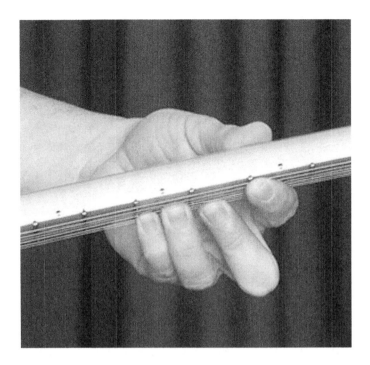

The trick to make a good "chord chord" is to place your thumb in the center of the neck and just behind the index finger, so you can put more pressure on the chord.

The palm of your hand should never touch the neck of the guitar; you should put your fingers on the frets according to the diagram we have here. As you can see, the vertical lines are marked by the strings of the guitar while the horizontal ones mark the frets.

C Major (C)

Play Track 12

The major C chord has the following position:

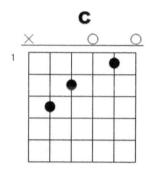

The 6th string has an X, which means that the string should not be played either in the air or in any fret. We cover it with our thumb. Let's put the ring finger on fret 3 of the 5th string.

We are going to put the middle finger on fret 2 of string 4. Leave string 3 in the air, put the index finger on fret 1 of string 2, and leave string 1 in the air. We do not want string 6 to sound, so we are going to cover it with our thumb. You must practice the chord very slowly so that each of the notes sounds as clear as possible.

D Major (D)

Play Track 13

D

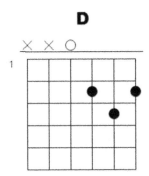

In this chord we leave the 6th and 5th strings covered and mute. Remember that our palm should not touch the neck of the guitar. We play the 4th string in the air, and with our index finger we play fret 2 of string 3. With our ring finger we play string 2 in fret 3, and with the middle finger we play fret 2 of the 1st string.

E Major (E)

Play Track 14

We proceed with the E major chord. In this chord we play the six strings of the guitar.

E

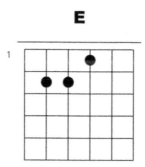

We are going to leave the 6th string in the air, with the middle finger in fret 2, the ring finger in fret 2 of the 4th string, and the index finger on fret 1 of the 3rd string. The 2nd and 1st strings go free.

F Major (F)

Play Track 15

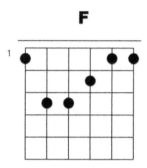

Then comes the interesting part: the "F" chord is a barre chord. That means we will position our index finger in such a way that it presses all the strings of the 1st fret. It should be attached to the fret, but not on top of it, so the strings can sound more easily. We're going to put our ring finger on fret 3 of the 5th string, our little finger on fret 3 of the 4th string, and our index finger on fret 2 of the 3rd string.

G Major (G)

Play Track 16

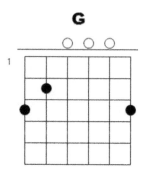

We can make the "G" chord by placing the middle finger on fret 3 of the 6th string, and the index finger on fret 2 of the 5th string. We leave the 4th and 3rd free, put the ring finger on fret 3 of the 2nd string, and put the little finger on fret 3 of the 1st string.

A Major (A)

Play Track 17

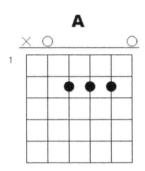

To play the "A" chord we will not play the 6th string; we will cover it, "crushing" the hand subtly against the strings that you do not want to sound. Leave the 5th string free.

Put the middle finger on fret 2 of the 4th string, the ring finger on fret 2 of the 3rd string, and the little finger on fret 2 of the 2nd string.

Leave the 1st string free. Remember, it is important that the palm of the hand never touches the neck of the guitar; it must remain in the air and leave a space.

B Major (B)

Play Track 18

Let's look at the next chord, "B." It is also a barre chord. We are going to use the index finger as a support, starting with the 5th string. The 6th string will not be played.

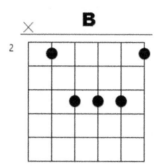

We put the middle finger on the 4th fret of the 4th string and the ring finger on the 4th fret of the 3rd string. The little finger goes on the 4th fret of the 2nd string and the 1st string must play on fret 2, thanks to the index finger.

C minor (Cm)

Play Track 19

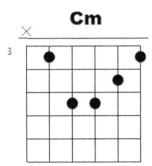

Now let's look at the minor chords, starting with "Cm." Let's do a barre chord on fret 3 from string 5. We are not going to play the 6th string.

Put the ring finger on fret 5 of the 4th string, the little finger on the 5th fret of the 3rd string, and the middle finger on the 4th fret of the 2nd string. Our index finger, in the barre chord, must press fret 3 of the 1st string.

D minor (Dm)

Play Track 20

Dm

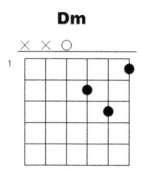

Let's look at the position of the D minor chord. We leave string 4 in the air, and the middle finger in the 2nd fret of the 3rd string. We put the ring finger on fret 3 of the 2nd string, and the index finger on fret 1 of the 1st string. Neither the 5th nor the 6th string should sound.

E minor (Em)

Play Track 21

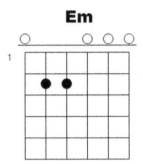

For the minor E chord we will leave the 6th string in the air. This one is going to sound. We'll put the middle finger on the 2nd fret of the 5th string, and the ring finger on the 2nd fret of the 4th string. The 3rd, 2nd, and 1st string are free.

F minor (Fm)

Play Track 22

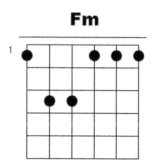

We play the Fm chord the same way we play the F major chord, but we remove the middle finger. We raise the index finger, and everything else remains the same.

A minor (Am)

Play Track 23

Am

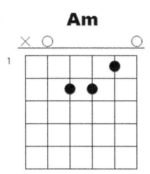

For A minor, we play the 5th string open and the 6th string does not sound. We put the middle finger fret 2 of the 4th string, and the ring finger on fret 2 of the 3rd string. With the index finger we play fret 1 of the 2nd string. We don't touch the 6th string.

B minor (Bm)

Play Track 24

Finally, we play the "Bm" chord like the Cm chord, but on fret 2, without touching the 6th string. We put the ring finger on the 4th fret of the 4th string, the little finger on the 4th fret of the 3rd string, and the middle finger on the 3rd fret of the 2nd string. Our index finger plays fret 2 of the 1st string.

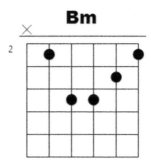

Now we have the major and minor chords of each of the notes. I'll give you a rhythm, so you can play something with the chords. You can do it with your hand or a pick.

You will play all the strings of your chord: down, up, down, down. Let's try it with each of the chords. If you want to hear how each one sounds, listen to the corresponding track.

If it gets too complicated or your hands or fingers hurt, then dedicate a day to a single chord. For example, try to make the C chord sound perfect today. You can make it more dynamic using the rhythm that we mentioned above.

Seventh Chords

Play Track 25

I will include some seventh chords. There are several of these, including the seventh major and seventh minor chords. Here you will see the most common ones.

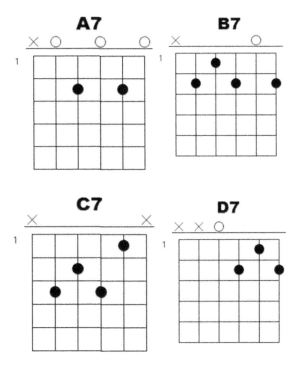

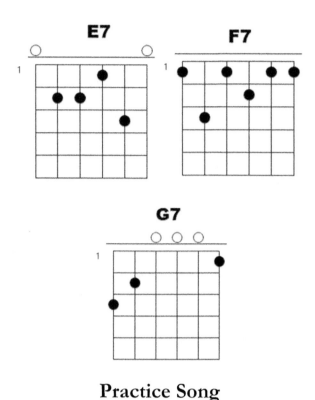

Practice Song

Now, we will put everything you've learned into practice with three well-known songs.

First, search the internet (YouTube, Spotify, etc.) for the songs you will practice. Listen carefully. Follow the lyrics and feel the rhythm.

Then, in the book you will find the lyrics and tablature for each song. The chords are located above the lyrics and they change as indicated.

Attached to each exercise you will find two tracks. The first one is a sample of how to play the song, so you can follow the rhythm and the sequence of chords. The second one is the song without a guitar; you will practice freely with it when you get familiar with the chords.

1. FOR WHAT IS WORTH - Buffalo Springfield

Intro: / E - - - / A - - - / (x2)

*Play Track 26
and Track 27*

VERSE 1:

E   A
There's something happening here
       E   A
What it is ain't exactly clear
         E   A
There's a man with a gun over there
        E   A
Telling me I've got to beware

CHORUS:

E (hold ½)   D (hold ½)
It's time we stop children what's that sound
A (hold ½)   C (hold ½)
Everybody look what's going down

/ E - - - / A - - - / (x2)

VERSE 2:
E   A
  There's battle lines being drawn

```
     E                    A
Nobody's right if everybody's wrong
E                            A
  Young people speaking their minds
          E                  A
Are getting so much resistance from behind
```

CHORUS

/ E - - - / A - - - / (x2)

VERSE 3:

```
E                            A
  What a field day for the heat
```

```
E                                A
  Ten thousand people in the streets
          E                      A
Singing songs and carrying signs
          E                      A
Mostly say "hooray for our side"
```

CHORUS

/ E - - - / A - - - / (x2)

VERSE 4:

E   A
Paranoia strikes deep
E   A
Into your life it will creep
   E   A
It starts when you're always afraid
       E   A
Step out of line the man come and take you away

CHORUS

/ E - - - / A - - - / (x2)

End on E

2.KNOCKIN ON HEAVENS DOOR - Bob Dylan

Intro: / G - D - / Am7 - - - /
       / G - D - / C - - - /
        / G - D - / Am7 - - - /
        / G - D - / C - - - /

Play Track 28
and Track 29

G ($\frac{1}{2}$)   D ($\frac{1}{2}$)   Am7
  Mama, take this badge from me
G ($\frac{1}{2}$)   D ($\frac{1}{2}$)   C
  I can't use it anymore

G (½)   D (½)   Am7
   It's getting dark to dark to see
G (½)   D (½)   C
   Feels like I'm knocking on heaven's door

CHORUS
G (½)   D (½)   Am7
 Knock Knock Knockin on Heavens door
G (½)   D (½)   C
 Knock Knock Knockin on Heavens door
G (½)   D (½)   Am7
 Knock Knock Knockin on Heavens door
G (½)   D (½)   C
 Knock Knock Knockin on Heavens door

G (½)   D (½)   Am7
Mama put my guns in the ground
G (½)   D (½)   C
I can't shoot them anymore
G (½)   D (½)   Am7
That long black cloud is coming down
G (½)   D (½)   C
Feels like I'm knocking on heavens door

CHORUS

End on G

3.WE DIDN'T START THE FIRE - Billy Joel

Play Track 30
and Track 31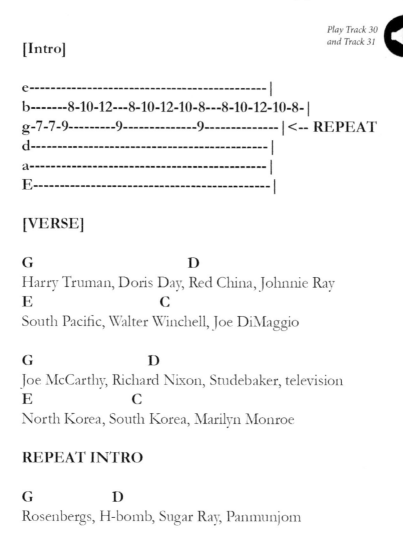

[Intro]

```
e------------------------------------------- |
b-------8-10-12---8-10-12-10-8---8-10-12-10-8- |
g-7-7-9---------9-------------9-------------- | <-- REPEAT
d------------------------------------------- |
a------------------------------------------- |
E------------------------------------------- |
```

[VERSE]

G   **D**
Harry Truman, Doris Day, Red China, Johnnie Ray
E   **C**
South Pacific, Walter Winchell, Joe DiMaggio

G   **D**
Joe McCarthy, Richard Nixon, Studebaker, television
E   **C**
North Korea, South Korea, Marilyn Monroe

REPEAT INTRO

G   **D**
Rosenbergs, H-bomb, Sugar Ray, Panmunjom

```
E            C
```
Brando, The King and I, and The Catcher in the Rye

```
G            D
```
Eisenhower, vaccine, England's got a new queen
```
E            C
```
Marciano, Liberace, Santayana goodbye

[CHORUS] (PLAY THE INTRO)

We didn't start the fire
It was always burning
Since the world's been turning
We didn't start the fire
No we didn't light it
But we tried to fight it

```
G            D
```
Joseph Stalin, Malenkov, Nasser aand Prokofiev
```
E            C
```
Rockefeller, Campanella, Communist Bloc

```
G            D
```
Roy lin, Juan Peron, Toscanini, dacron
```
E            C
```
Dien Bien Phu falls, Rock Around the Clock

G   **D**
Einstein, James Dean, Brooklyn's got a winning team
E   **C**
Davy Crockett, Peter Pan, Elvis Presley, Disneyland

G   **D**
Bardot, Budapest, Alabama, Krushchev
E   **C**
Princess Grace, Peyton Place, trouble in the Suez

[CHORUS]

G   **D**
Little Rock, Pasternak, Mickey Mantle, Kerouac
E   **C**
Sputnik, Chou En-Lai, Bridge on the River Kwai
G   **D**
Lebanon, Charlse de Gaulle, California baseball
E   **C**
Starkweather, homicide, children of thalidomide

G   D
Buddy Holly, Ben Hur, space monkey, Mafia
E   C
Hula hoops, Castro, Edsel is a no-go

G   D
U-2, Syngman Rhee, payola and Kennedy
E   C
Chubby Checker, Psycho, Belgians in the Congo

[CHORUS]

G   D
Hemingway, Eichmann, Stranger in a Strange Land
E   C
Dylan, Berlin, Bay of Pigs invasion

G   D
Lawrence of Arabia, British Beatlemania
E   C
Ole Miss, John Glenn, Liston beats Patterson

G   D
Pope Paul, Malcolm X, British politician sex
E   C
JFK, blown away, what else do I have to say

[CHORUS]

G   D
Birth control, Ho Chi Minh, Richard Nixon back again
E   C
Moonshot, Woodstock, Watergate, punk rock

G   D
Begin, Reagan, Palestine, terror on the airline
E   C
Ayatollah's in Iran, Russians in Afghanistan

G   D
Wheel of Fortune, Sally Ride, heavy metal, suicide
E   C
Foreign debts, homeless vets, AIDS, crack, Bernie Goetz

G   D
Hypodermics on the shores, China's under martial law
E   C
Rock and roller cola wars, I can't take it anymore

[CHORUS]

We didn't start the fire
But when we are gone
It still burn on, and on, and on, and on

Being a Rookie

Learning to play the electric guitar is not easy. Everything is new, you have many questions, and there are a thousand ways to make mistakes. In this chapter we will discuss some potential mistakes and give you the confidence to buy your first guitar.

Errors

Note: When I use the terms "left" and "right" I do so based on a person whose dominant hand is the right one. If you are left-handed, remember to invert the terms when reading this article.

Mistake #1: Needlessly Rotating the Fingers of the Left Hand

This is the most common error among rookies. They play with the fingers of the left hand (the hand that treads the strings on the fingerboard) tacked or inclined towards the body of the guitar.

When you tilt your fingers that way, you remove extension to fingers 3 and 4 (ring and pinky). Therefore, you will have to make a sudden change of position if you need to use those fingers to play notes on the thicker strings (for example, a note on the 5th or 6th string with the little finger), which is inefficient.

When this error is not corrected, the rookies stop using the little finger. Why? Because having the fingers inclined makes it more difficult to use the little finger, since it is farther from the strings than others. Therefore, consciously or unconsciously, they avoid using it when playing. By not using it, the finger does not develop strength or agility.

Mistake #2: Pushing the Strings When Stepping On Them

This error is also quite common among rookies, especially when they begin to play their first chords with capo. They push the strings (usually downwards) when stepping on them to play a chord or a note.

By pushing the string, you detune the note. In addition, it is likely that if you push too hard, you will touch an adjacent string, which may prevent it from emitting its sound.

This problem occurs due to lack of sufficient strength and control in the fingers. The novice guitarist usually does not have enough force in the fingers to step on the note. So, he or she compensates by making more effort than necessary and pushes the string out of place in the process.

Mistake #3: Sticking Your Hand to the Body of the Guitar

This error is common among rookies who begin to practice fingerstyle. It consists of gluing the edge of the palm of the hand to the top of the guitar. The problem with this position is that it severely restricts the movement of the fingers on the right hand. This prevents the hand from assuming an optimal position to emit a good sound.

By not having enough space to move the fingers, the rookie compensates by constantly moving the wrist. This destabilizes the right hand.

It must be remembered that, when playing fingerstyle or classical style, the movement that produces the sound does not occur on the wrist, but on the knuckles and fingers. The hand should remain in a neutral and immobile position.

To achieve this, instead of anchoring the hand to the top of the guitar, it is necessary to place it in a floating position, letting the fingers fall naturally on the strings.

Mistake #4: Tilting Your Right Hand Up

This error consists of placing the right hand on the strings, so that the palm of the hand is facing upwards. The problem with this position is that it leaves less space for movement to the ring and little fingers. As a result, you will get a weak and unbalanced sound.

In other cases, it causes an explosive sound due to the tendency to pull the string with the fingers. The palm of the hand should be facing towards the guitar and not upwards. This way, all the fingers will have the same space to move, thus facilitating the production of a more balanced sound.

Mistake #5: Tilting the Pick Too Far Down

This is a common mistake when doing practice exercises with the pick. This position causes two main problems.

By tilting the pick down, you will naturally favor the "downstrokes." That causes the sound of the notes that are pressed downwards to be stronger than the "upstrokes." The product is an unbalanced sound. In addition, this makes it more difficult to execute even rhythms (for example, eighth note and sixteenth note rhythms).

Tilting the pick down offers great ease for downward movements, but resistance to upward movements.

Choosing an Electric Guitar

The most complicated part of being a rookie is choosing an electric guitar that not only meets the technical needs for learning, but also fits your budget. There are three questions you should ask yourself before choosing an electric guitar.

How much are you willing to invest?

You can find cheap guitars and expensive guitars. The budget intervals usually are as follows:

$100 to $280

$280 to $600

$600 and up what kind of music do you want to play?

If your style of music is pop, indie, or blues, guitars like Fender Telecaster, Fender Stratocaster, or Gibson are good choices. If you are looking for a heavier sound, you want a model like LTD, ESP, or Washburn.

Do you want to learn to play the guitar for a while or be a guitarist?

If you're simply looking for a hobby, it's not necessary to get a super guitar. If this is the case, I recommend that you buy an electric initiation guitar. Try an economical one and experiment.

Some examples of brands like this are Memphis, Squier, and SX, and some models are Strato, Telecaster, and Les Paul.

Memphis Stratocaster - black

However, before buying a cheap guitar, I recommend that you check a series of technical aspects: that it has no lever, that it has a fixed bridge, and that the mast is glued and not screwed. The less complexity in a beginner's first guitar, the better. You should also pay attention to the frets, whether they are brass or not, and that there are not a few frets higher than others, since this will cause the string to fret. It is also important to analyze whether the tuning fork is straight or curved.

Famous Guitar Players

Six Great Electric Guitar Players

Every guitarist has his or her idols, and some of these stars might be on your playlist. Listen to them to immerse yourself in their music.

Jimi Hendrix

He does not need an introduction. This great guitarist influenced a whole generation of musicians and will continue to influence the next. Although he died at age 27, he had time to develop many new techniques in his short and impressive career.

BB King

The king of Blues inspired great musicians such as Eric Clapton and Jimi Hendrix. He knew how to express his passion. I want to pay homage to this musician who left us in 2015.

Eric Clapton

Singer, composer, and guitarist, after playing with the Yardbirds and the Bluesbreakers, he released his style, which was influenced by Blues. His fans call him the Slowhand in reference to his technique.

Carlos Santana

Carlos Santana has made his style of Latin Rock known to the whole world. He often collaborates with international stars.

Keith Richards

An essential member of the Rolling Stones, Keith is Rock personified. Accompanied by Mick Jagger, he still plays the songs of this historical group today. Keith Richards is one of the most important guitarists in the world.

Chuck Berry

Every self-respecting rocker reveres this man, who was one of the originators of Rock and Roll. He wrote famous songs like Johnny B. Goode, Sweet Little Sixteen, and Maybelline. The world continues to consider him one of the greatest guitarists of all time.

Unlock Your Musical Potential: Get 30% Off the Next Step in Your Instrumental Journey

As a token of appreciation for your dedication, we're excited to offer you an **exclusive 30% discount** on your next product when you sign up below with your email address.

Click the link below:
https://bit.ly/40NikR2
OR
Use the QR Code:

Unlocking your musical potential is easier with ongoing guidance and support. Join our community of passionate musicians to elevate your skills and stay updated with the latest tips and tricks.

By signing up, you'll also receive our periodic newsletter with additional insights and resources to enhance your musical journey.

Your privacy is important to us. We won't spam you, and you can unsubscribe anytime.

Don't miss out on this opportunity to continue your musical journey with this special discount. Sign up now, and let's embark on this musical adventure together! 🎼